A Schizophrenic's
Life & Advice

STEVEN MAX ELDER

A Schizophrenic's
Life & Advice

TATE PUBLISHING & *Enterprises*

Published by Tate Publishing & Enterprises, LLC
127 E. Trade Center Terrace | Mustang, Oklahoma 73064 USA
1.888.361.9473 | www.tatepublishing.com

Tate Publishing is committed to excellence in the publishing industry. The company reflects the philosophy established by the founders, based on Psalm 68:11,
"The Lord gave the word and great was the company of those who published it."

Book design copyright © 2008 by Tate Publishing, LLC. All rights reserved.
Cover design by Stephanie Woloszyn
Interior design by Kellie Southerland

Published in the United States of America

ISBN: 978-1-60462-922-4
1. Self-Help: Mental Help: Schizophrenia
2. Biography & Autobiography: General
08.03.26

If we dwell over our own mistakes,
we have no courage and strength
to face adversity. I lived with faith,
and now have life to grow with God.

by Steven Max Elder
November, 2006

Acknowledgments

I would like to extend some thank you messages to the men and women who have given me hope, inspiration, friendship, love, and support. The following are my words of my remembrance for every one of you who gave me your knowledge to better my life.

I would like to thank my grandmothers for their upholding faith in God and their raising me a Christian. We went to church and ate meals afterward with good conversation and enjoyment. I will never let a chance go by without recalling your words, Grandmother, on behalf of my grandfather who died months before I was born: how Grandfather, as you said, would be very proud of me. Although my grandmothers have passed over to heaven, I will never forget your love and hugs. I love you all.

To my many friends who held me high and proved to be faithful in my darkest times, I write you the truth that there is a second family, and this is you, my dear friends. I miss you, but like you, I am doing what you have always had the confidence in me to do: succeed and fulfill my desires in life. You all have so blessed me, I hope someday we can all be together to celebrate my new, reborn life in Christ. I have to tell you all I am still a sinner, but I am now saved, thanks to you, my dear friends, for making me keep my faith. You're all family.

To President George W. Bush, and to his presidential correspondent, I thank you for always receiving the letters I have written and responding to them on behalf of the president. You have given me a gift.

I would like to thank my psychiatrist, Lisa Schmid, M.D., for being intelligent enough to have found a medication that has given me a maintainable life. I give you my word, a promise of compliance with my medication. I thank you for your faith in me, your hopes, desires, and encouragement to continue my education. It takes all of life to learn what life is really all about, but the door of knowledge opened, and when it opened, the light of knowledge set me free. Thank you.

My anthropology professor, Bernice MacAlister, is foremost among those who helped me accomplish my book. She told me in a letter that I would go on to great success. She also knew somehow that I would write a book. Remembrance of you brings me life, and our vision of my future has come to be reality.

I would like to thank my parents. As I like to write, you have the gift to read. Here is my first book. Thank you for the support and love, also life! I know I have been a turtle when it comes to a life with a family of my own. However, Dad and Mom, marriage is in my life plan. Be patient.

Thank you to my sister, Jennifer, for always encouraging

me to write. Since you say I write like I speak, I hope you enjoy my first book.

Linda Burgess, I thank you for you devotion and friendship. I want to write thanks to you for editing the first draft. You have been a consistent support of this book and I am grateful for all your help. God bless you.

Contents

Foreword

As a practicing psychiatrist, I have treated hundreds of patients with schizophrenia. I have also read extensively on the topic of schizophrenia in order to keep abreast of new medications and therapies. I have seen this disease up close and observed the range of tools that patients employ to try and live with such a complex syndrome. This book is one man's story, and serves as an unofficial guide to truly living with schizophrenia.

Steven Elder's book relating the unfolding of his life stands out as a refreshing and novel look at the day-to-day experiences of a man with a serious disease. Most people have no sense of the reality of living with mental illness in general, or schizophrenia specifically. Those who do know are the families and friends of patients and the mental health professionals who treat them. People tend to be afraid of these patients because they don't understand their disease process and don't have the practical information to make them more knowledgeable. This causes separation and isolation for the person living with schizophrenia. Steven has bridged this gap by opening the door to a life that most have never seen.

Steven Elder's story is a clear, straightforward accounting of his life that does not attempt to hide the difficulties he faces every day. But it is also a very personal story about a very special human being. Beginning with the diagnosis that he at first resisted and denied, Steven takes us on an intimate journey that brings him, finally, to the acceptance of his condition allowing him to become the success he is today.

I hope this book will give those families touched by schizophrenia some much-needed hope where they may not have experienced any before. People living with schizophrenia will find a new friend, a wise guide who understands this challenging road and has transitioned from merely surviving to really living.

So, I say to Steven: continue to carry on bravely. You are already my hero. To those who are courageous enough to read this book: may Steven become your hero, too.

Dr. Lisa P. Schmid, M.D.
Claremont, CA

Introduction

My name is Steven Max Elder; I am the author of this book for schizophrenia patients. In answer to the requests of my family members and my psychiatrists, I have constructed a well-thought out plan to help schizophrenics who would like to read in private about our experiences with this mental disorder. I have learned how it is possible for us to live rewarding and abundant lives despite our illness.

In 1984, I was a twenty-two-year-old college student—full of energy, hopes, and plans—when I was diagnosed with schizophrenia. My doctors allowed me to read their diagnostic reports and hospital notes about me, and I was frightened. "How could a doctor know that much about me after only a five-minute interview?" I asked. I wanted the doctors to be wrong. I began to read the only resources that were available when I was first diagnosed: technical books that described symptoms and predicted limited improvement. Those books made me even more afraid. Reading caused me to silence myself. I wished for a sympathetic, optimistic, non-technical source of information. Today, schizophrenia patients still have that need, and I have attempted to fill the void with this book.

Luckily for me, my parents could afford a clinical psychologist for therapy twice a week, and I had permission to call whenever anything needed resolving, whenever I became caught in the moment with so many questions, trying to find answers as to why I was experiencing these voices in my brain. The schizophrenic symptoms and the schizoid personality seem to arise at unpredictable times and sometimes all day and night.

This book devotes chapters to different topics that you may need to understand. At any one time, maybe only one paragraph or chapter will interest you. However you feel about reading this book, please know that it was written with my compassion and my desire to find a way to communicate to those who have schizophrenia that there is hope. Each life is unique, and medications are becoming more advanced, more resources are available, and research continues to find new ways to treat schizophrenia. I try to give the person dealing with schizophrenia assurance that you can achieve some stability, depending on how severe your disorder is, and how you deal with symptoms.

I place tremendous emphasis on medication because it is the only treatment that can bring you to a minimal level of maintenance against the disorder of schizophrenia. Therapy with a counseling support person such as a psychologist or marriage and family therapist is, in my experience, a good way to gain information about how to find ways to cope with and prepare a plan for how you will react to voices, hallucinations, depression, paranoia, isolating yourself from people, or talking to the voices you are hearing in your brain. These are symptoms we as schizophrenics have to deal with day after day.

PART ONE

About Me, Today

Hello, and thank you for reading my book.

I would like to introduce myself by telling you a little about me. I am forty-five years old. I live in Claremont, a southern California city near the San Bernardino Mountains. I have an A.A. degree, and I am now a student at California State University, San Bernardino, majoring in theatre arts. I am a registered pharmacy technician in California. I have attempted to patent an invention. I have written and copyrighted lyrics for country and western songs. I am a living advocate for those with schizophrenia.

It has been a difficult path, living with schizophrenia. My heart, soul, and prayers go out to you who live with schizophrenia. I too hear those troubling voices and see those hallucinations. I have battled the difficult decision about whether it is necessary to take medication even if it works only some of the time, and I still have schizophrenia with medication. But I am an advocate of medication and the way it can benefit the brain when you follow the directions on the bottle that contains your unique prescription given to you by your psychiatrist.

I hope you will find the information to help you achieve your highest level of success, and I hope that my experiences help you, possibly by relating in some way to your own daily experiences with schizophrenia. Your successes will be different than mine because you are unique.

I believe that no schizophrenic can go without medication and a supportive psychiatrist. It's mandatory for success and ultimate self-control to learn how to have a plan in place in your brain when the symptoms of schizophrenia do become active. As much as there is controversy over IQ scores, your intelligence is different than mine, different than everyone else in the world. So never have feelings that you're not smart. You are unique in every way, and that is something to be proud of: your own presence on earth.

I believe that the assistance of a psychologist or marriage and family counselor can be very effective in dealing with reality and finding ways to cope with schizophrenia. I have written this book to be a friend, as a way of giving you even more support, to help you as an additional resource when you are dealing with voices, depression, hallucinations, and paranoia.

Now that I have become aware of my symptoms, I can and do work and go to school. I find time to walk, ski, ride my bike, lift weights, go to church, and sing in a choir. I enjoy my life by applying a new truth to the unreal voices that many times we hear. I just know they are not true, and the only means of communication are verbal or written, in person or by computer, e-mail, or telephone. There is no mental communication for schizophrenics; this is illusion. Sometimes you may just take a deep breath and remind yourself that these voices are false. You don't have to say it aloud, but the thought in your brain can be enough to help you control yourself, so that you don't bring attention to yourself. Understand that the voices are untrue. In time, with practice, you will do it naturally.

I hope you enjoy the book.

Medication

This chapter is devoted to medication compliance, the most important part of my book. Schizophrenia is a serious and incurable mental disorder, but it is treatable. There is nothing in the world that can help a patient with the diagnosis of schizophrenia more than continuing a psychiatrist's prescription of a medication to be used as a treatment.

The best solution I have found is that your currently prescribed medication is always better than no medication at all. Please remember that your doctor can't read your mind. If you think the symptoms of hearing voices, seeing hallucinations, talking to the voices, anger, agitation, dry mouth, constipation, vomiting, paranoia, suicidal thoughts, or harmful thoughts of others are present, please contact your psychiatrist without delay and make an appointment. *There is help.* Your doctors are trained to deal with any situation you may have, but you must tell them truthfully if you have been discontinuing your medication, or if you have used drugs, alcohol, or cigarettes. These four situations can greatly alter the delicate chemistry and physiology of the body. Remember, any of these can cause you to have the symptoms of schizophrenia.

However, if you have been compliant with medication and not abused substances that are harmful when mixed with medications, you may need an adjustment to your medication, or in severe cases, you may need to be placed on a different medication that will help relieve some of the characteristics associated with the disorder of schizophrenia.

Never take more than directed. The body is sensitive, and if you take more or less medication than prescribed by your psychiatrist, you could change the delicate chemistry of your body. Please take your medication only as directed. This will cause the medication to work correctly. There are many decisions that go into the prescribing of your medications. The psychiatrist must consider your weight, and volume of your body. That way, you receive the correct amount of medication for your body. Also your history of mental illness is considered, what medications work, and your doctor, after reviewing your history, may find that there is a different drug for the treatment of different symptoms you are having. But what ever you do, take the medication according to the prescription instructions. This is the main defense for anyone diagnosed with schizophrenia. There is truth that schizophrenics who are on medication do better than those who are not. A leading cause of hospitalization is going off medication. So do yourself a favor and keep taking your medication.

Whatever the reason for a new medication change directed by your doctor, or the decision to try a new medication, it is best to take what is prescribed by your own psychiatrist. Be always truthful with your doctors about your habits and the symptoms you are having; this is the only way they can help you reach a functional level of self-maintenance. What do I define as self-maintenance? It is the ability to work and better educate yourself when you have resolved all the issues you are working on with your psychologist, marriage and family counselor, or therapist. With this consistent support of a psychiatrist and compliance with medication, you may find yourself accomplishing tasks you always wanted to complete. Find your desire and fulfill it with success. Whatever desire you have, reach for your highest success.

But this all takes the right medication that is prescribed for your own physiology and personal psychology. What motivates you is achieved only when your problems are resolved and you are taking your medication as prescribed. Remember: never act as an amateur psychiatrist or psychologist when it comes to taking your medication or treating your own schizophrenia. You can consider this to be a best friend's advice to you. I was never able to succeed until I recognized that I was schizophrenic.

I would like to give you a scenario of what happens when you discontinue taking medication, or abuse drugs, alcohol, and cigarettes when taking medication. It may seem to you that you are feeling fine, or perhaps someone tells you that you do not need your medication, but the fact is, if you stop taking your medication, you are setting yourself up for failure.

The drugs that your doctor prescribes are the only drugs that you should take. Although you may wish to feel different and may wish to self-medicate with other drugs, that combination is a prescription for disaster. Street drugs and alcohol are addicting, and if you start using any type of street drug, it will affect you the rest of your life because every time you abuse drugs, you are destroying part of your physiological and psychological body.

You have to also understand that your prescribed medication may lead to major dysfunction when used with street drugs. It's a known fact that the combination of street drugs and medication and alcohol will greatly increase the possibility of overdose, cardiac arrest, permanent brain damage, or death. It's no joking matter to say "I am high" to a friend. In my experience, it is the fastest way to self-destruction.

There is no way to have a productive life addicted to drugs. Drug dealers do not want you to know the truth; drugs take away from the quality of life you once enjoyed before drugs. They do not want you to know that they and you are a team set out to die. They will take your money and let you pay to die.

The world won't grieve for you if you die a drug addict. Do you want to be remembered as someone who died of an overdose? The world will remember men and women who help others because they are the force of earth trying to make life better. The best is always remembered.

Hospitalization

I cannot expect you to believe me unless I share with you the dark side of my own life. At the age of forty-five, I have finally begun to understand it.

There were so many people telling me I was schizophrenic when, like you, I didn't believe I was schizophrenic, and my behavior wasn't severe. I had a job and a girlfriend, and I attempted junior college. But there was always someone telling me, "Take your medication."

I want to write about the dark times when I struggled with being hospitalized. Schizophrenics rarely discuss how we feel personally the feeling of the mental hospital units that so many of us know. I know the sensation of being given no freedom in a closed unit in a hospital and being forced to comply. If I desire to move into an open unit, I still must remain until the psychiatric staff reviews my records and release me. It's a place where no one wants to spend the rest of our lives! It's full of ugly experiences that we keep to ourselves or share only with close friends or a significant other. We find that they agree; it's not a place we should be placed into. But if we have a conservator who has been given legal permission to be the authority over our health, that person has the right to keep us there. Some conservators may even have the right to make all our financial transactions, giving us a small portion of our check to live on. If you are in this situation, your payee has real authority over you, and there is nothing you can do to change your feeling of being controlled. The control is real, and the pain is great, especially while you are locked up in a hospital or a mental health center. I feel sorry for you who are in this situation. How many times in my own situation I hoped someone would let me be released, but the psychiatrist had the final word!

If you are in a hospital, I am sorry for you. I know it's a test of faith that there is a God who will help in this time of need. It's a difficult test of being forced to take medication and obey rules and have privileges given and some taken away. How helpless we can feel! There is nothing I can do or say other than that I am with you all the way, and believe me, taking medication is what you are there for. It is a difficult test of patience to trust, but taking medication is the only way out.

I was twenty-two years old when I was first diagnosed. I had been in psychotherapy. Then, one year later, I was asked to go to a mental hospital in a city close by where I was living. There is no choice, only the compliance to medication and remaining calm for the time you are hospitalized. You also have no choice but to be a courteous as possible with the staff if you desire to be released early. I know this is difficult because everyone seems to know all about you and your illness; however, the reality is that they don't know. You have to wake up and make this time useful and rely on the only treatment proven to relieve symptoms of schizophrenia: medication.

I was hospitalized several times during my twenties even though I was in therapy. I was taking medication and still hearing voices. I continue to this day to be puzzled by these situations. I was at home, and the doctor came by with my father and came into the house, and they were saying that I was schizophrenic, and guess what happened. You got it; I was hospitalized by my doctor, who had the authority to place me in a mental hospital because he believed it would benefit me if I were on medication in addition to psychotherapy. They had the idea that this was the best place for me to be. All of a sudden, I found myself in a locked unit where I was observed behind glass by nurses, psychologists, psychiatrists, and psych technicians. I remained under observation for a week to ten days. I was told I must spend time in the main room, not my bedroom. Talk about difficult! It's hard to imagine what they were writing about me even when they would not be speaking. All the patients in this closed unit were under observation. I know that the doctors were billing insurance and had to write down a diagnosis so that insurance would approve coverage.

A few years later, when I was twenty-eight, I was living and working in Stockton, California, at a business that was very successful. I was feeling good, and I stopped taking my medication. I had worked there several months when I made the decision to move to New York to seek a career in theatre. It didn't occur to me that I needed to go to college and study acting first. It didn't occur to me that I might need to save up enough funds for my relocation.

Well, I made it to Albuquerque, New Mexico. I was determined to make it farther, but I was out of money, so I found a room to rent. I got a job at a mom and pop restaurant. The only problem was that my earnings were less than my rent. It sounds funny now, but at the time I was suffering from the environment, and I was losing touch with reality. At night the place was thick with cockroaches all over my room. I would tuck myself into the sheet and make an all-sided cover for myself to keep them off. I had no money; I had no choice. To make a long story short, I ended up calling my old employer in Stockton for a chance to work again. He agreed.

My family and friends could see what was happening to me, and they kept telling me to take my medication, but I didn't think I needed it. I had no money, so I sold my car, and I bought a bus ticket back to California.

When I arrived at the bus station, I must have been in a bad way. My family urged me to go to a hospital, to get balanced, to get back on medication

Well, the most difficult time in my life happened in Stockton State mental hospital. One day in section A, that's what they called the room, a patient who had really no reality and was extremely angry turned over a table. One psych tech and one nurse began yelling at him to put the table back. I knew he had no reality, so I put the table back up. The next thing I experienced was the two yelling. They grabbed me under the armpits and put leather straps around my wrists and ankles, laying me face down on a wooden restraint table. I remained there more than six hours. All I know is they moved me to another section when the doctor found out. He asked me if I would like to take Valium. I said, "It's addicting," and I asked another medication that was not addicting be given. The doctor agreed.

On the fifth day I was there a judge and a panel of men and woman confronted me and asked me, "Do you have a place to go to? If you don't, would you like to try our program to establish yourself until you find work and your own place?"

I found a job and ended up staying in the same building where I had lived before I went on my roundabout trip to that mental facility. So I learned, and it took many a long night to understand, that if I had only taken my medication I would have never been placed in such a horrible facility. The major lesson I learned was to trust God because the truth prevails, and reflecting back, stay on my medication. The entire experience at Stockton State Mental Hospital was the most difficult way for me to face the reality that I had no choice but to stay on medication. I know now that it is the only successful treatment for schizophrenia. It's best to take what helps you live a productive life. So God bless you in your most horrifying hospitalization. Believe me, He does exist, I have my own life as proof.

Managing Your Care

It often seemed to me that I was admitted to a hospital because someone was making a profit on my care. The doctor even convinced my family, who was paying $10,000 for two weeks. I realized after being with this doctor that there must be a way to find better help for myself.

I finally found at age thirty a doctor who was able to treat me in a county-run facility that didn't benefit from hospitalization, and it was rarely used. My doctor was Filipino, and her compassion helped me meet my goal: graduating from Chaffey Junior College.

I have had both male and female doctors, and I have found that what works for me is a female psychiatrist. I'm looking for support in my desire to maintain with as few problems as possible, and I want to make my own judgments about daily life. I have found female psychiatrists to be nurturing and sympathetic rather than controlling.

It is best is to be choosy about who you see because there

are as many methods as there are doctors. So be looking for someone who helps you, who accepts messages if you want to share on a particular day, and who requires you to visit no more than needed—once or twice a month. My doctor works around my schedule and her own. Many times we do not see each other for eight weeks, giving me a chance to work out my own problems if I have any. My doctor wants to make me independent, which is best for mental health. I know there will be mental health professionals who disagree, but you are paying for care even with Medicare. They have money to gain and lose if you choose someone else. Do not become trapped in therapy with a doctor or counselor. You are best advised to find a good doctor in private practice. You pay cash, and are not billing insurance; therefore privacy is maintained.

Some insurance carriers will pay only for terminal illness and that may not be your situation. It helps if you have doctors who share what they write about you. That's solving the problem of keeping everything open in conversations between you and your doctor. You should be able to review your doctor's notes so that both of you take equal roles in addressing a particular diagnosis. This strategy keeps improvement in mental health at its highest level.

Do not misunderstand me. Mental health workers and professionals are not working against you. If they were, they would be exposed and restricted from receiving their license to practice. But the system does not always work in your favor, either. So maintain as much control as you can. Clarify what you need and what way can you obtain it. Say to yourself, "I shall succeed in all my goals." That's a good attitude to maintain for all your life.

If you can, stay away from or ignore those who are downers about the abilities of schizophrenics. I guarantee that what they are saying is that you are not capable of success because you are schizophrenic. Mental illness has been treated horribly throughout history. We can look back at thousands of years of treatments, each accepted at its specific time in history of the world. Some treatments were better than others, but people in our situation have always suffered from discrimination and negative stereotyping in addition to the symptoms of our disease. So take charge of your life, and really think about the situation you are in with mental health professionals. Find all the best available support. Then take time to question those who are not really adding to your self-esteem, the ones who drag you down. Get rid of these people and find someone better. You will probably confront anger at first, but you have the right to see who you want when you pay cash for office visits. But let me warn you, if you do pay cash and change doctors, it is their wages that they will really be thinking of. They may discourage you or give the old guilt trip because your money is leaving. You need to take care of yourself, and if someone who is treating you is not working, find someone else. There are plenty out there to choose from.

Maintaining an Awareness of Self

I would like to share my own life education on how to maintain an awareness of self. I have an Associate of Arts degree in theatre from a junior college in

California. I was accepted by the American Academy of Dramatic Arts in Pasadena, California. I am currently enrolled at California State University, San Bernardino. I have two more years of work ahead of me to complete my B.A., and then I may continue in graduate school.

Now that I have given you some background of my academic work, let me relate it to the chapter title. As a theatre student, I have taken classes in body movement and acting. When I began studying theatre in college, I was highly aware of the visual symptoms of schizophrenia. You can imagine the effort that was inspired by knowing that I must be the best to succeed in the theatre department, if I desired to act. Only the most dedicated students received continual success at auditions.

What I learned is to place myself in a room and to imagine that I am everyone else in the room looking at me, at my every facial expression and body movement. You too can do this. Observe yourself while you are by yourself, and then try this practice in a crowd. Record your observations about yourself in the notations section at the end of this chapter. Then become aware of how you are sitting and whether your mouth is open or closed before eating. Have you any new truth to write down about how you are different when you realize how you are noticed by others? You can now correct any behavior that may be a symptom of schizophrenia. You may notice you stare, or speak and laugh, have paranoia, or hear voices. All of these symptoms can affect your body from the inside out.

This practice is called self-awareness. It's hard to accept at first, but with practice you can change your outer presentation of yourself to a behavior that would be considered normal by any psychiatrist who understands body language. Wait, don't panic! I know you must continue to tell the truth to physicians that treat you for schizophrenia and must continue to take your medication. However, this exercise is designed to make you aware of any symptoms that are visually or audibly recognizable to represent schizophrenia.

You can place yourself by imagination into the viewpoint of people around you and see how they are looking at you. There should not be paranoia in this exercise because no one knows what is in your brain but you. ESP does not work in schizophrenics, nor in the majority of the world. So if you hear voices, it's all in the brain. Do not become embarrassed by your effort to become aware of your facial and body movements when you are in a room with others or by yourself. This exercise is designed to keep what goes on inside your brain inside so you do not talk to yourself alone in public and laugh alone, or have paranoia of others because you hear voices. Those experiences are only symptoms of schizophrenia.

Try breathing through your nose and then keeping your mouth closed while you are alone in public. This awareness will help you to not talk to yourself. In another way of putting it, delusion is all in your brain. Although it's really happening to you, a schizophrenic, it is abnormal, and a mental illness, and part of schizophrenia.

So look in the mirror at your face and remember everything about your face visually. Then close your eyes and try to recall what your face looks like. If you can do this, great! Do not worry if it takes a while; we all have different abilities and experience. Practice getting to know your face and what it looks like to you. Then try closing your eyes and recall what you look like with the power of memory in your brain. It's fun when you get the memory in recall.

These are just a few ways that you can become aware of yourself with schizophrenia. There is nothing to fear. What I am giving you are ways to keep the mental symptoms of schizophrenia inside so they do not appear as physical abnormalities. No one who is diagnosed with schizophrenia intentionally wants to be abnormal. That is why it's important to praise yourself for what you accomplish when you master self-awareness. Then it will seem as if you are, by appearance, like everybody else in the crowd. You and your family, close friends, and doctors will know that you are schizophrenic, but the overwhelming mental symptoms will go not noticed by the untrained eye. There's nothing wrong with being and appearing normal; most schizophrenics are doing it already.

Although I didn't realize it as a child, my mother and father believed that I could accomplish anything I set my mind to. I continue to this day remembering my mother sitting me down at the breakfast table and telling me I could be any occupation in the world. She began listing some titles I could achieve such as doctor, lawyer, congressman, or senator. I may not be any of these at this time in my life, but one or two are still possibilities. The reason I am sharing this with you is all that of these careers require self-awareness. Think of how professional people behave around others most of the day. They must maintain a personality that is free of their feelings and remain pleasant to all they meet in order to function in their jobs.

So, actually, we are all doing self-checks on ourselves throughout the day. In some ways this practice is conscious, but it is done so quickly that we do not realize we are even doing it.

However, Self-awareness is not present for many with schizophrenia because so many of the symptoms remain inside the brain, and the inward illness affects our verbal and visual perception of how we relate to the world. There are some who live in hospitals with very low awareness, and others who are extremely aware of all they are doing every moment.

Here is another method of being aware: notice how we dress each day. In college I was able to take a course on the history of costume design. I learned how clothes not only give clues to our social status but influence how others think of us as men and women. Throughout history, clothes have become a way to understand what level of economic wealth or social class a man or woman occupied. You would never see a man who was a farmer in the field wearing the suit of a gentleman. So, before you dress each day, think of how others notice new clothes, and forget older, more common attire for the day. There is no need to be angry about this. It is life, and the majority of the people in the world are influenced by awareness of self. When we see someone in distinctive clothing, any of us will probably react. Clothing sets the first impression of how we are presenting our self to others. Let's face it; clothes make an impression no matter who you are. They establish how others will react to you.

I also took a course in children's theatre. Think of the impact that the actors and actresses had upon these young children. Children are always taking in through the senses what they are experiencing, as this is how we learn. The children knew how to react to a man who wears distinctive clothing like a prince or a villain. So there is more to self-awareness, and as schizophrenics we must learn all about maintaining an awareness of self.

I have invited you in this chapter to share some methods I use to overcome the internal schizophrenia that we know influences the external body of schizophrenics because of what is happening inside the brain. I hope some of this information will guide you to techniques that you may use to overcome symptoms such as talking to yourself, mannerisms of facial expressions and body language.

This information is not absolute; I have developed this technique over a period many years. Do not feel you are never going to succeed. As I have told you, we are all unique and have different ways we can accomplish what is in this chapter. You may do as I hope and start slowly until you see who you really are in the mirror. Then remember to view yourself with your eyes closed and practice this technique. Learning this practice does not have to be fulfilled in one day. Take your time and enjoy these new techniques.

Personal Notes on Self-Awareness:

Look in the mirror: what do you see?

_____

_____

_____

Close your eyes and remember your face.
What do you see?

_____

_____

_____

What is your posture like?

_____

_____

_____

What clothing have you received compliments on?

_____

_____

_____

Carry on Bravely

There is nothing more difficult than living with schizophrenia. Although there is no cure yet, there is progress being made. Living with schizophrenia is the most difficult life that I can imagine because even though research is ongoing, there is no cure for this mental disorder. When you are diagnosed with schizophrenia, I understand the frustrating feeling of not knowing whether there will ever be a cure. The average schizophrenic may deal with many difficulties. Many times with schizophrenia, all anyone can do is show love for those who are suffering from this mental illness. I compassionately say to you who suffer from schizophrenia that I extend my deepest feeling to you; there is hope for success in the future when you realize that you are not alone.

Medication and therapy truly can help, but I realize there are many times that you provide the only support for ongoing symptoms and daily side effects. Those are the days that we have no doctor appointments and we must live the best that we can when dealing with the difficulties of the day. I know how hard it is to deal with, and I have words to help: *Carry on bravely.* I had a college professor speak these words to me every day as I left her anthropology class. Those words were very motivating to me; they made me feel that no mater how tough my day was, I always had the courage to live each day strong in spirit and strong in health. I became the master of my life.

I never worried if I slipped and my brain wandered, if the subject was boring in the classroom. I knew that no one knew. As a schizophrenic pursuing a college education, I have found that my appearance on campus is much like that of a living actor. I practice being aware of all my facial expressions and aware of keeping quiet until someone is speaking to me so I don't walk around campus speaking out loud while walking to class or in class. I just listen as well as I can, and I manage in class better than many expected. I won honors in anthropology, and I am now majoring in theatre. I now look back and am thankful for the hours I studied each day for years to complete my degree. I was motivated to be the best and appear humble so that others would feel comfortable being with me even though I am a perfectionist.

Living with schizophrenia and having a psychiatrist as a friend is the best possible blessing because your doctor gives the most valuable assistance. Financial support greatly depends on family income and whether you have the ability to hold a job and keep it. Although there are Social Security disability, state disability programs, and government insurance, being self-supporting and paying medication co-payments can be very costly in addition to doctor visits. Then your situation is complicated by pressure to achieve, or by those who think you never will achieve anything. My advice is that you begin by rallying support for your desire in life.

Then it will be proof that makes others believe in you, so if you say you're going to do something, then follow though with your desire. For you and me, it's the old cliché: "If at first you don't succeed, try, try again." These are good words to live by. If you have tried to do something and you did not follow through, try a different approach to accomplishing your desire; this time you just might succeed.

I would like to suggest that you try a task that isn't difficult to accomplish. After you have completed this task, try another one that is a little more difficult than the last. This process will give you self-esteem to continue trying to gain that ultimate quest to be self-supporting. There is no greater feeling than accomplishing your own desire. But remember to be patient with yourself because some tasks take longer than others to accomplish and succeed. In my own experience, I always find happiness in trying to find out how infinite my abilities really are, and I have only the limitation of my own desires. Realize you may not be what others are, but you may find a unique path that leads you to fulfill your life desires in a happier way.

I realize there is still prejudice in this world against schizophrenics. I have listened to the jokes and the fear of people living with schizophrenics in their community, but only uneducated people think schizophrenics should be feared. There was a church-sponsored housing project in a city where I once lived. The community protested so much that when I was at the city council meeting, I, like the church, couldn't believe the false statements being made by the men and women of the city who objected to our presence. Why would I live in a city of such people? I made a decision to move away from that city. Although some men and women may have false beliefs and fears about schizophrenic, I hope they realize that schizophrenics can obtain college degrees, and have and hold onto jobs. These are the men and women who help relieve the world of prejudice against schizophrenics, and are the people that work for the good of others. This has been my own experience.

I believe that as more and more patients write books on schizophrenia when they are educated and receive college degrees, that some of the false beliefs about the men and woman who have schizophrenia will disappear. I hope we can be accepted as valuable men and women who have the ability to overcome prejudice and prove our ability to succeed as teachers of our own experiences with this treatable disorder. There may not yet be a cure for schizophrenia, but there are medications that can treat the symptoms. This is good knowledge to remember. Patients who do not accept medication to use in the treatment of schizophrenia act out the abnormal thinking and behavior of schizophrenia, and cause difficulty for all schizophrenics.

I believe that I have overcome adversity with my own strength and courage to face those prejudiced men and women, and prove that I am successful at many tasks. I have motivation to show my success and prove to my adversaries that their fears are not true. If you can understand how many great men and woman have overcome great burdens and had belief in themselves to achieve what they desire, then you are on the path with me, trying to help those who are schizophrenics, and people who know schizophrenics as well, overcome their blind prejudices and find out the truth about schizophrenia.

Like most who live with an illness, we as schizophrenics must rely on our doctors' advice. This should be your first choice when it comes to advice. I know in session

your situation is private, and your doctor is your confidant. Cherish this unique relationship.

There will never be anyone else who will know your problems and find ways to treat them as well as your doctors. They have the highest level of education to assist you with any difficulties you are having because so much of your schizophrenia is treated with medication. However, life can be very blessed with the help of your doctors; they are your best friend when it comes to treatment. The best advice I can give you is listen to your doctor, who knows your true abilities and can be a source of support that you will not find in many situations in life. Your doctor is capable of being a friend when he or she is given the truth by you. Whoever you choose to treat you, make this relationship, like every relationship, one to uphold with a great deal of trust and honesty.

Personal Notes

One small task I would like to accomplish:

_____

_____

_____

One way that I succeeded today:

_____

_____

_____

Schizophrenic Blues

This is a chapter about depression or as I like to refer it, "The Schizophrenic Blues." This is not a clinical name recognized by psychiatrists, but rather a name I created to describe some of the depression schizophrenics deal with every day. How do men, woman, and children deal with the pain and suffering that accompanies depression along with schizophrenia? I would say the first step in dealing with depression is to recognize the signs of depression by asking your doctor. If you do have depression, your doctor is the only one who can prescribe medication for depression. Sometimes depression can be physiological, dealing with the body physically; or it may be psychological, caused by events or situations from the past and present. If it's physiological, maybe your brain is not producing chemically what it needs, a situation that can cause the brain to malfunction from happiness to depression. Just as you are different from anyone else, so will be your schizophrenia and depression; you may or may not have it as severely as others.

Your doctor will prescribe appropriate medication, judging whether the reasons for your depression are psychological or physiological. Depression can be genetic, and you are not to blame. But with all its mysteries—as the old cliché goes—life is not always walking in a rose garden and smelling the sweet smell of the roses. So take life as it is, and if you are suffering from depression, tell your doctor. Please report any changes you may notice, since these can be side effects of the medication you are taking. If you are unsure that you can explain the changes alone, ask your doctor or pharmacist. Do not ever feel you are bothering them; this is what they are paid to do, so feel free to ask questions about your medication. You may at some time experience mood changes, dry mouth, constipation, anger, aggression, or sedation; this is not a list of all the effects, so please ask your doctor or pharmacist about side effects.

Next, you may be asked by your doctor as part of your treatment with medication to seek a psychologist, marriage and family counselor, or therapist to help you with your feelings and give you methods you can use to overcome the pain of depression. There are an enormous number of techniques to use in therapy. I know there will be one that is right for you. Life is hard when dealing with depression alone. So do not believe that there is no way to resolve the problem with depression.

Most schizophrenics have at one time or other had some form of depression. It's no good feeling down about anything. I know that there is in your memory a time you can remember when you were feeling happy; for example, Disneyland, and the fun of the excitement of the rides, all the people in costumes, and the parades. I am sure that you can think of some time when you were somewhere that you were feeling happy and joyful. When you feel overwhelmed, try to remember a place of happiness, and use your brain and concentrate for a moment on this happy time. This at first may seem difficult, but with practice it becomes easier. I am not a substitute for good therapy. I can, though, assist by sharing what I have learned about depression through the years, and help you find a way to resolve and restore self-power over depression.

Life has had at least some happy moments, so try writing memory cards. Take a 3 x 5 blank card, and write down any idea you come across that might help in dealing with horrible thoughts from voices you are hearing, voices that can trigger stress and make your mind resemble an abusive person telling you how worthless you are. Remember your cards at this time, if you are able to safely (not while driving a car or operating machinery). Put that memory into your brain, and remember that it is not true; the voices are not really your enemy or friend!

Some situations such as molestation, rape, or verbal and physical abuse require a trained mental health professional. Do not ever feel ashamed or afraid to discuss anything with your doctor or therapist. This is what they are trained to do for a living. These professionals are here to help, and they want you to feel happiness once again.

If you feel suicidal, call your doctor and follow the procedures requested, and go to a hospital emergency room for help. If you can't reach your doctor, hang onto the knowledge that you are important, and so is your life on this earth. You can call 911 emergency and tell the operator that the reason is that your medication is not working, or you have not been taking it correctly. There is immediate help by calling 911. You have only one thing to remember: hang in there; it may

STEVEN MAX ELDER

be tough now, but the chances to have a better life depend on you knowing the truth. It's only an episode of abnormal depression, and there is a treatment to help.

Before I give you some situations of resolution for depression, I would like to say there is no more valuable known treatment than anti-depressants and good therapy with a trained professional to deal with depression. Its success is based on monitoring, and the best advice is to never go off your medication because most anti-depressants take a period of time as long as two to three weeks before they begin to work. Discontinuing medication will make you feel depressed again. Do yourself a favor, and take all your medication at the same time each day and try not to miss a dose. Take exactly what is prescribed; taking more or less will not be following you doctor's advice. Remember the medication can do only so much, and therapy may be advised.

I do believe that you will never succeed until you have accepted that you are schizophrenic. This is the real truth that will set you free to then begin to realize that there are others in this world who have schizophrenia. The key to their success is that they have accepted that they are schizophrenic, and that life could have been more difficult with thousands of more severe conditions. The fact is, schizophrenics with depression have life.

Researchers are coming closer every day to finding new medications to deal with both of these disorders. How lucky you are to be schizophrenic with depression in this time in history! Even though you may find daily life difficult, there is tremendous support from federal, state, and private organizations that are helping men, women, teens, and children with money to help life become easier for those with schizophrenia and depression. What a wonderful life you can claim with medications that treat almost every symptom of schizophrenia and depression!

The truth is that non-compliance is still the main problem; however, the longer you are on medication, the greater the chance you have allowing yourself to find out that life is not that bad after all. This discovery will give you a whole new life to experience. You can work, or go to college if this is your desire. The path must be well thought out. Take one step at a time. One easy job or class builds confidence to try something more difficult. Until you begin to succeed, there is never a feeling of accomplishment. But it is possible, if this is your dream, desire or goal.

I would like to add that there will be the possibility of depression as a schizophrenic with the onset of voices, hallucinations, paranoia. There is help out there, and as I have written, it is best to tell the truth of depression and realize the cause and find help.

Personal Notes on Overcoming Blues

Describe a time when you were happy:

_____

_____

_____

How can you bring that same joy into your life today?

_____

_____

_____

Set a small goal for improving your life:

_____

_____

_____

Voices

Most all schizophrenics have listened to voices and claimed they are either in the brain, or sound like they are coming from outside the brain. Voices can be triggered by large crowds, when you are alone, or almost anywhere. If you believe that they are really someone else, disregard that belief and know that it's the brain functioning abnormally and it's part of life as a schizophrenic. They are not really people talking to you with the use of ESP or mental telepathy. The effects of voices can be a horrible burden to bear. I hope this chapter helps you find a way to deal with the voices as I have.

Voices can be listened to even in a mental hospital. How many men and women in a hospital, who have been off their medication and are just beginning to take medication again after a long period, think that there is ESP or mental telepathy going on in the hospital? Well, I can say it's quite a large number. The truth is that your brain is not functioning normally, and you are probably a little confused if you believe that the nurses and doctors are causing the voices. There is no ESP, and you must not believe that they are using any means other than verbal communication to bring you back to normal. It takes time for medication to work successfully. I know that there are many situations that can bring you to a mental hospital; however, one common one is when you stop taking your medication. I know that for many of us the voices will never go away, even with the use of prescription medications. I can say that I would rather take my medication than end up in a mental hospital because I made a decision that the medication was not working, or the excuse I was fine without it.

Why do you end up in a hospital having your own private thoughts but thinking that everyone is aware of your thoughts? I tell you with all honesty that this is untrue. No one knows what you have going on in your brain until you decide to get help, and you should not fear discussing with your doctor the fact that you are hearing voices. You must realize that you are hearing voices because of this horrible abnormality of the brain.

I live with voices every day of my life. There has never been an appointment with my psychiatrist that the subject of voices has not come into conversation. What makes me unusual is that I know that hearing voices is an abnormality associated with schizophrenia.

When I began my college education, I realized I had a talent for acting. I became aware of my movements as well as other people's movements. I also learned that the audience does not know the reality of what goes on in my brain. I can perform in a two-hour musical and remember every laugh line and script that has my lines and rehearsed movements—and be listening to not only the actors but to voices in my brain. I have the blessing of proof. I can walk out on stage and it becomes my reality. However, when I leave the stage, my reality is just me with schizophrenia. I learned to be aware of my facial expressions, composure, and all the other actors' mannerisms. I won a scholarship in theatre in college, and I know that if they only could have my brain, they would understand me and never would have given me supporting roles because of what goes on in my brain and the voices I was hearing when I was delivering a line. But the audience always laughed after a funny line, or applauded after every scene I was on stage. I learned a lot about how others judge us by our behavior, and I am one man who was gifted to always to be in control of facial expressions, movements, mannerisms, and most importantly, educated how to act as an actor and after the scene still return to my own self. I have learned in acting that my character is either fictional or non-fictional. With this knowledge I can maintain who I am after a scene of production. I can easily change to a man and keep busy so I do not have to just sit and listen to voices. I fill my days with work, exercise, meditation, moments of praise to God for life, and always a personal relationship with Christ.

While I was in college I also had the opportunity to direct students in a production. I knew that I was respected as an actor by my peers, so I used my best ability to pick the best actors and actresses available. The production was a success.

I learned to let the actors develop their own characters. This gave them all the freedom and faith that I was given when it came to creating a character from the script. The personality and description came from information according to the script. Anything else—mannerisms, facial expressions, character's voice—came from the actor. The movements I made on stage came from the director and choreographer. What I am suggesting to you in this para-graph is that no one in this theatre setting ever knew I was schizophrenic because I was just myself offstage and in character onstage. The transition was easy for me, and it did not take a really difficult amount of work to be able to return to myself and to be my own unique self. What I am every day when I am in classes or being with friends is different than on stage. I finally had the proof that no one ever knew that my abnormality of the brain was causing me to listen to the voices in my brain. I had the ability to remember my lines and movements, and stay in character, regardless of being a schizophrenic. It was a relief to me to discover the ability I have to concentrate on what was being said—and to know that what was going on in my brain wasn't reality. There was nothing to fear, for I had found a way to deal with voices and schizophrenia.

I would like to try and explain to you how important it is that you explain to your doctor what life is like for you when you are hearing voices. I have a wonderful psychiatrist who knows that I hear voices. But in my thoughts, while this is going on, I remember that it's a characteristic of schizo-phrenia. I have thoughts regularly in my mind to discard what is being said. I know that I am the only one who can turn those voices into background noise with the help of my prescription medications. I am lucky that I control the voices with the help of medication, and I do not believe what the voices say. I alone know the truth that every day is different, and the voices change each day. Over the past twenty years, I have developed the ability to recognize that this abnormality is decreasing as I build my own ability to manage its distraction. I am developing the power to find resolve in knowing the voices are false information. I just ignore them and concentrate on the other communication available; communication that is the reality of the majority of men and women who do not hear the voices.

I would like to close this chapter by asking whether you have a successful method for dealing with voices and a method for not believing what the voices are saying. If you are not harmful to yourself or anyone else and have a method, and if there is any additional information gained from this chapter, we are on the path to success. There is no better way to get over the embarrassment of what the voices might be saying to you.

Remember the voices are only going on in your own brain and no one else hears what you hear. Whomever you associate the voice with, you must know that you are not really hearing this person. If you can believe that the voices are not ESP or mental telepathy, then you are crossing over into the brain patterns of men and women who have overcome delusion.

If you desire more information than what I have briefly written on voices, a good source of information is your physician, psychologist, or mental health professional. They can guide you best in methods of treatment. It took me many years of struggle dealing with voices to progress to the day that I was able to write a book on my own schizophrenia. I give anyone with schizophrenia my highest regard because we live in a world where there is only treatment and no cure. However, we can do our best to live a productive life given financial support, education, good health habits, and medication.

Most of all, I did not get to where I am now by believing that I was disabled, or by accepting that I am unable to achieve all I choose and desire in my life. I was determined that I could make a better for myself and others. This resolve has always been a driving force in my life. I am not a man who gives up when everyone around me says I am unable to do something. I just ignore them and go away and accomplish my goal, then return with the ultimate reward: I have fulfilled my desire, and have proven I am truthful. There have been many men and women who have helped in the path of direction I follow, and they have assured me that I am intelligent man.

I believe there will be many amazing successes in the cure of schizophrenia in the decades to come. What a wonderful hope and prayer!

I close this chapter with a few words of support for you as a patient with schizophrenia. You are a blessing of God. Your life is important, so strive to achieve self-maintenance, and when all your personal needs are accomplished, go and do something to help someone else in the world. A free gift comes from a good soul.

Light

What I would like to accomplish in this chapter is to bring you into the light. This metaphor you may initially interpret as religious. If you are thinking that this is one of those books that guides you into a spiritual awakening, that assumption is just not true.

I am not educated to give any more than my personal knowledge of faith in God, and this story is my own journey through my life's experience. If you need to know, I'm a believer. I strongly encourage you to seek the wisdom of any of the religions in the world by method of reading or researching online, and to listen to those who have been blessed or educated. Now you understand that I am no minister.

I am not claiming to save your life and bring about a miracle to you through the reading of this book. I promise only that it is the truth to the best of my ability to make sense of schizophrenia to average men and women who have never read a book written by someone with this mental illness. Expect no persuasion into religion here. I am nothing more than a writer. Languages and culture are different everywhere, and I accept your good beliefs.

I am no new discoverer either. I leave scientific investigation of schizophrenia to doctors, pharmaceutical companies, psychologists, and other mental health professionals.

Stepping into the light is more of a personal decision to comply with your psychiatrists' wisdom, to end the problem of not accepting their knowledge that you must stay on medication. I use the figure of speech "stepping into the light" in this chapter to give you a comparison of two situations so that you may find a choice to make.

Here is the first. I have revealed to you that I struggled with medication compliance through most of my twenties and thirties. But then came the day that I stepped into the light shining in a room, and I asked myself, *If I were going to die tomorrow, what have I done in my life?* I looked at myself and I saw that I complained and did not listen to the many doctors who told me, "Medication is your only hope." Well, it's the truth.

If you are not like me, if you have stayed on medication, then I commend you. That is the best blessing you could give to yourself. But what I have noticed is that schizophrenics in all age groups have at some time or other stopped taking their medication. When we stop, it is only a matter of time before we begin to show symptoms of schizophrenia. It happens to all of us who are schizophrenic. It's not acceptable. As I am sure you have found out when you stop taking your medication, there are going to be those that recognize a change in behavior. They may tell you to listen to them, but the only way to overcome this abnormal behavior is comply with medication. Yes, this far from what you expected this chapter to be about, but as you shall read, I stand with mental health professionals that the main treatment for schizophrenia is medication prescribed by a psychiatrist who specializes in the treatment of schizophrenia.

I know that you may be one of those who has always complied, or the opposite, you never accepted your medication; either way you know that over a long period of time schizophrenia changed your behavior. Voices, hallucination, paranoia, depression, or schizoid behavior: these are a few symptoms of what can happen when you go off medications. The desire to stop arises because medication may build up a tolerance in your body. This means that the level of medication over a period of time decreases its strength in the body. So visit your doctor regularly and tell the truth. Do not lie to the doctor when a symptom comes up because you do not want to take medication. Share your feelings with your doctor. You may need to be placed on another drug that has not been introduced to the body before, and has the right amount of medication to relieve you of the desire to stop taking your medication. It's all true. I know that in mental health, psychiatrists, psychologists, nurses, and therapists can guide you on the path to take your medication. They are all trained. Believe me, your parents want the best for you, and only desire the best for you if they truly love you, but one person that you can always rely upon is your psychiatrist.

So join me and step into the light if you have not done so already. It's a good feeling to share my words with you, and I hope that you will take this book as a equal: me the writer and you the reader.

Hallucination

A majority of schizophrenic patients experience hallucinations. What are hallucinations? Seeing or hearing something that does not exist in reality. In this chapter I will give situations of hallucinations to help you to understand what hallucination is ... and that you are not alone. Different patients will experience different severity in how often they have hallucination, and the type of hallucination.

I would like to ease fear so that you can discuss your experience with a trained psychiatrist or mental health professional. I know how hard it is to tell doctors what you see or hear. However, there is nothing to fear. Your doctors are aware that this can happen to schizophrenics, and they are the only resource to help you realize it's not reality and there is help. Hallucination is common to schizophrenics, and why this happens is unknown. If you see something in your sight that appears to be visual, but at the same time you know that it is something that is usually not discussed openly, this is hallucination. I hope that when you finish this chapter that you will not feel alone as the only man, woman or child who has had this experience.

I will include some examples of hallucinations to help you understand. Even if these are not exactly what you have seen or listened to, they may make you realize that you are not alone when it comes to hallucinations.

I will begin with a fictional situation that may be a similar delusion to one that a schizophrenic may have experienced. You are in your car, and you are driving, and months earlier you have stopped taking your medication. While driving, you are hearing voices and you continue to recognize that the voices are not true. The medication that you were taking for several years is still in your system; however, you are aware that everyone is telling you to continue taking your medication; they fear that you will be hospitalized because you are off your medication. Although you feel that your reality is the same, you are driving away from where you live and believe you are doing just fine. You insist to everyone that you do not need medication and that you will not have a relapse. Then it happens. You have been relying on God to help you maintain without medication. You have been not experiencing normal sleep behavior; you stay awake for hours, and you rise at day light. Your brain is beginning to stray from reality. Then as you do not believe there is a problem, you see Christ in the distance. You are confused and do not know whether to believe that it is Christ or not. You see him fade away, and the experience is over in less than a minute. You then begin to believe the best: that it is Christ in reality. I can guarantee you that you will struggle with this and that at some point in time you will fear speaking of this situation to your doctor.

So time goes on, and then the worst happens: you think you see Satan. Now you have begun to relapse from your medication, the hallucinations are overwhelming, and you pray and start talking to God and Christ to make Satan go away. But the vision only persists over a longer time. This is an example of a visual hallucination, and if you have ever had a hallucination of God or Christ it could be a pleasant experience; however, if you think you have seen Satan, you can be sure that it would be a very unpleasant experience. Because you are disturbed by this vision of Satan, you begin to speak out loud your thoughts, but you are not able to control speaking out loud when you see this hallucination. This you keep to yourself, and others begin to ask you who you are talking to. You reply in a defensive way to cover up the fact that you now realize you are being noticed for this change. You fear someone calling you schizophrenic. However, after you have become not functional at work, or don't pay your bills, or can't maintain independent living, you find yourself back in the hospital. The doctors place you on medication, and you begin to regain reality.

What you can learn from this sequence of events is that you may hear voices and have hallucinations, but medication has control over your sense of reality. Yes, if you are having hallucinations, it is far better to tell the truth and get the medication available to relieve the stress that delusions may cause you. If you become preoccupied with your mystical experience, this is a symptom of schizophrenia. Please, if you have ever had a hallucination, do not fear telling your psychiatrist. You will be doing yourself a big favor because your doctor is aware that schizophrenics can have these hallucinations. Fear not, there is help.

Here is another situation of a form of hallucination. Your family member dies; let's say it's your grandmother.

You were very close to her and you miss her pleasant ways of how she would call you names like "honey," "sweetheart," "dear," "love," "sunshine." You have been in your brain having thoughts of her after her death, and you so want to believe she is in heaven with God. There is nothing abnormal about this hope and belief.

You pray and desire that God will save her, and in prayer you ask him to bless her for all the nice times in your life with her. Then you remember hearing her voice. However, you have not been taking your medication, and you begin to hear her voice. This can be an auditory hallucination, and if it is discomforting, it can then be a very difficult to live with. The chances are you can remember hearing her voice telling you all the wonderful words she had to say about you. But this is only one possibility. You may remember a bad situation with a family member who died. The voice you hear may be disturbing and cause you to suffer at the sound. In this case the auditory hallucination can become more of a burden than a blessing. If this is the case, that there are bad memories and that you relive them when you do not want to, this illusion can lead you to develop a sense that your relatives are continuing what they did when they were alive. This is a horrible situation to deal with all alone. If it persists, you should not fear telling your psychiatrist or mental health professional about what you are experiencing. Your doctors have experience with dealing with loss of family members, and may prescribe medication and suggest counseling methods that will be right for you when dealing with the death and loss of a family member. There is nothing to fear. There is help out there for you. This type of hallucination can possibly lead to problems of reality.

From hearing the voice repeatedly, you may develop a doubt whether it is just a delusion in your process of thinking. You could develop a complex problem, so the sooner you deal with hallucinations, the better you will feel.

Paranoia

Paranoia is a diagnosis. You may have been told that you are a paranoid schizophrenic. Paranoia is a change in your thought process where you may say in conversation that you are going to be something like, "I am going to be a famous actor or actress." This belief is considered to be a delusion of grandeur. You believe that you can be a famous star, though in reality you have no training in acting, and never follow through with this desire. Logic argues against your dream because there is no way to predict success and fame. I hope you understand that although someone begins saying he or she can be a star, no one ever can predict stardom.

Here is another delusion of grandeur. Let's say there are people who have been diagnosed as paranoid schizophrenic, and they expect to marry someone famous and become wealthy men or women. Although they have no education and money, they believe that they can fulfill this desire. Then after treatment with medication, they return to a non-paranoid personality and realize that they can not accomplish this, and that they have suffered from delusion of grandeur. So delusion of grandeur is simply expressed as a temporary thought disorder where the patients leave a state of reality, believing that they are capable of accomplishing great success, though they have no education or power to fulfill their delusion. Delusion is a brain dysfunction where the patient leaves reality, and thus believes he or she can do something that will never happen.

Paranoia can also be a fear or suspicion that you are being followed and there is no real truth to this; however you believe in your brain in people you are not able to decipher between reality and non-reality. This delusion fortunately can be treated with medication and counseling so you can realize the truth that you suffer from schizophrenia, and that the paranoia is not true.

Here is another scenario of paranoia. Let's say that there is a patient who is panicking over the success of another person. The patient has the belief that this person is going to be wealthy, famous, marry some woman, and the patient is worried because she thinks her acquaintance is gay. The patient is panicking that she must stop this person from succeeding. This is a patient who is paranoid schizophrenic because there is no proof, but it's a belief in the brain that it is true. For the most part, treatment with medication and counseling will help bring the patient back to reality, help him or her recognize that this was a delusion, and after treatment, the thoughts and fears pass away in time.

For the patient with paranoia, this can be a very difficult time because the problems that arise with the onset of paranoia many times require the patient to be hospitalized because the patient could harm to his or her self or someone else. When the patient becomes medicated with anti-psychotic medication and monitored by mental health professionals, the brain becomes stabilized with the function of reality.

I would like to write some more situations of paranoia, in the hope that at the end of this chapter you the reader can understand paranoia, as well as what is reality. There is a patient who has paranoia; he believes that he is a genius and that he is going to be famous and wealthy. To complicate his delusion he believes that he is in danger and fears that someone is trying to kill him. When he tells this to his doctor, he is diagnosed paranoid schizophrenic. They discuss his belief and fear, however, the patient fears for his life and offers information to prove he is a genius. The doctor who has known the patient for many years asks the patient if he is a genius; the patient's reply is yes. When the doctor asks the patient what makes him a genius, his reply is, "I have a secret invention and no one can know about because you wouldn't understand." The doctor calms his patient down and begins by firmly telling him that he is suffering from delusion of grandeur and paranoia because he is a paranoid schizophrenic. The patient is asked to go with the doctor to the local mental hospital. The patient is fearful of the hospital; however, with persuasion, the patient enters the hospital where he is assured he is safe. Here we have a situation in which the doctor knows the patient is delusional and paranoid that someone will kill him for his secret. Reality is that the doctor has known the patient for years, understands the patient is not genius and not in danger of being killed, but is a risk to himself.

Let's say there is a patient who has for a few years taken herself off medication. She is now homeless and living in the streets and sometimes in shelters for the homeless. The patient was on medication for several years prior to discontinuing her medication. But now she is in a state of mind with no reality. She cannot take care of herself, but because she refuses help, finds herself in and out of police stations. She sometimes is asked if she was ever mentally ill, and her reply is no. Although she denies that she has been in treatment and been in a mental hospital, she will not take her medication. She begins to have melancholy feelings and becomes depressed. She turns to alcohol to kill her pain. Then it happens: a series of paranoid beliefs. She thinks the police are trying to take her to prison, and begins hiding behind trash cans and drinking until she passes out. But each day she awakens with paranoia.

She looks suspicious, someone calls the police, and she is diagnosed paranoid schizophrenic after her interview with the hospital staff psychiatrist. Luckily for the patient, the doctor, who is compassionate, helps the patient relax with medication, and the devoted staff finally gets her to confess she has taken medication before. The patient meets with a social worker who helps her obtain Social Security benefits, assists her in the finding housing and food stamps that she is entitled to, and helps her find employment because the social worker recognizes intelligence. Even though the patient can not exceed working income in excess of $800 gross a month she now has two incomes, shelter and a new life. What saved this patient is the help of others, who gave her the security to admit she had taken medication before, and is now diagnosed paranoid schizophrenic.

Now that I have given you some case studies of paranoia, I would like to end this chapter with some information on what is considered reality when you are diagnosed schizophrenic. Reality is considered to be what is real: for example, you, a patient diagnosed with schizophrenia. That is true and reality. What is real is that we all have struggles and times of happiness, as well as times of sadness, such as the loss of a loved one. This loss would cause sadness. This is reality can be non-reality if your grief is so disabling that you require hospitalization over this loss. It then is diagnosed differently: possibly obsessive with compulsive crying, extending over an abnormal period of time. Reality in dealing with death is that it's natural to mourn the deceased because they have gone and you can not bring back to life. That is a true statement of reality.

Also, those who at some time have the desire to become something must remember that the only way is to go through the process others have gone through. The people whom you wish to be like have a specific level of training and education. If you accomplish your goal by proof and truth, then it then becomes reality. But if you say you want to work and attain independence, than you need to go through the process to become independent; then it becomes reality. If you tell someone that you would like to graduate from college, then there is a lot involved. First money, getting accepted to the college, filling out the financial forms, attaining housing and food plans on campus, and like many, continuing to work at a job, and earning passing grades in your classes. This is the reality of going to college. You can see how difficult it is, and you must also remember that you will need medication and a local psychiatrist, and that takes money. But if you do desire to go to college, then be prepared to follow all the commitments required to graduate.

There are rules to obey in the classrooms and the campus. But if this is your life dream, I believe that if you have an average level of intelligence, you can find a way to go to college. All that I have written on attending college is reality and truth. It would be delusional if you believed you would but did not have the grades to be accepted into a college.

I hope that I have given you the knowledge that you need to understand the difference between paranoia and reality. This is the most important information that I can give you. I must share my belief again, that we are all different—different intelligence levels, different personalities, different abilities, and different economic backgrounds. But we share many of the same privileges in life. I hope you understand these words of encouragement, "Carry on bravely in the face of adversity"; this means be strong in spirit, and be brave when others go against you, be patient and wise. There may be a problem, but I shall overcome my schizophrenia and find resolve in this truth, and then I will be on the road, to open the door, and to see the light of intelligence that awaits me.

Overcoming Stereotypes

How do I overcome the stereotype of schizophrenia? The first step to understanding your illness is that you acknowledge its existence. By admitting to your doctor that you are schizophrenic, you enable room for healing, thus you open the door to knowledge, information and education. Then you can discuss with your doctor symptoms of schizophrenia, and you can understand your doctor.

We have all heard the term schizophrenia. In the centuries before treatment became effective, there was great shame attached to mental illness. People who suffered from mental illness were locked up and hidden away by families who feared that their pain was hereditary or contagious. Today, the fact that there is no cure for schizophrenia still gives those who are not educated about this mental illness an opportunity to make false statements about it. The stigma continues today because of media portrayal of schizophrenics as violent or evil, or as having multiple personalities like Jekyll and Hyde. These are the lies that most schizophrenics deal with every day.

However, this stereotyping of schizophrenics truly is a lie. We may be disoriented; we may have difficulty judging the realism of our hopes and fears; we may have difficulty with social functioning; we may be discriminated against, but we are no more violent than any other segment of the population.

What has not been told by Hollywood hype or media exploitation is that there is a life that can be fulfilling with the diagnosis of schizophrenia! This is a truth known all over the world by psychiatrists and psychologists who have patients who live well each day with schizophrenia.

There are multitudes of men and women who have this disorder. There are children, teenagers, young adults, mothers and fathers, and grandparents. These men and women are what this book is all about: courageous individuals who are able to succeed with the support of psychiatrists, and counselors, with the help of medication to treat specific symptoms of schizophrenia.

So how does this disorder affect family? Schizophrenia can still be misunderstood because there still is no cure at this current time in history. There is also difficulty because the cost of the doctors, therapists, and medications can be a great burden on a middle class to poor family. The struggle to meet the expense is sometimes not attainable for many families. So a person who could be productive is shattered by the high cost of treatment.

I have found that many times drug companies will work with you and your insurance to make sure schizophrenics are able to receive medications at little to no cost. The best way to find out is to speak to your local pharmacists about savings and programs offered by your medication's manufacturer, and call the company directly. I have had this happen to me, and a pharmaceutical company assisted me by giving me medication at a reduced price based on my income.

The only treatment for schizophrenia accepted by most psychiatric associations around the world is medication and visits to mental health professionals. So for now we must trust available information. I hope that if I can help in any way it would be to guide you through my experiences and the faith that you will learn to accept the current treatment of medication compliance.

I know that the path is different for everyone, and I must have it easy if I can write a book on schizophrenia. But college education and years of trial and error have taught me that the chance to succeed is attainable. If you learn to accept help, then there is a way to treat what has so long been secret, that hidden word in our society. The taboo exists, but the chance to change this is available to all of us diagnosed with schizophrenia. Each of us offers a unique experience to share with this world.

We change the world by taking medication and setting an example as good people, being aware of ourselves and our appearance. These are simple ways that we as schizophrenics can present to the public a new view of what schizophrenia really is, thus reducing the discrimination that we might face. Some ways to change are accomplished by methods such as hygiene, taking a shower a day minimum, making sure we have shaved in the appropriate areas as men and women, and keeping our clothes clean and as close to current style as possible.

Because most schizophrenics are not rich, we must learn to budget money for clothes. We can find clothes in style without spending all our money. There are many stores that offer fashion at a discount. You may think stylish dressing is unnecessary, but the truth is that when we decide to make a change, we must present the best image possible. It is normal for middle and upper class citizens to buy fashionable clothes, but do not feel you can't appear in style while you are saving money. I know people's impression of you is built in a very short period of time from their first sight of you. There is nothing wrong with fitting in.

There have been people who have overcome greater obstacles and challenges in life than a schizophrenic will really ever imagine. Who and what could this type of person be?

Think of the famous woman named Helen Keller, who in her life faced some of the most difficult burdens to overcome. The next time you think you cannot succeed, think of Helen Keller. She was blind and deaf and could not speak; a child that many said was a waste of time to teach, when a mentor and a most compassionate woman, Anne Mansfield Sullivan, came into her life. Anne's patience and Helen's desire to learn made Helen an accomplished writer and advocate for the handicapped. Both of these women are inspirations for the world today.

Three schizophrenics who have made a great impact on the world were the extraordinary ballet dancer, Vaslav Nijinsky; the brilliant impressionist painter, Vincent Van Gogh; and Nobel Peace Prize economist John Nash, all men who exemplified self-discipline. They did their work in times when today's medications were not yet available, and so they suffered greatly. But they changed the world.

To break the schizophrenic stereotype mold, you need knowledge and understanding through education. This education can be high school, or college, or it may come from a professional trained in the mental illness of schizophrenia. You break away from what is seen as a disability and complete an education that will eventually make you self-supporting. This move is the breakthrough from the stereotypical mold of schizophrenia.

You may limit yourself by believing that you may never be educated, but I am a schizophrenic who has spent years trying to complete a bachelor's degree, and as I have written, I have been given a continuing education scholarship to complete my degree. I am just like everyone else. I did not ask for special privileges when I enrolled at college. This is what I call breaking the mold—working and going to school just like an average student. I know my limitations, and I believe that when we accept that there are students with disabilities who may require assistance, there is nothing taken away from their success. The path may be different for everyone, but I truly believe that with the right support and with health that is maintained, you will achieve your goal in time. It just may take a little longer.

There may be some of you who feel hurt when you read that the stereotype of a schizophrenic is not broken until you reach the level of self-sufficiency—mentally, physically, and financially. But, truly, this independence is what ending the stereotype is all about for schizophrenics. The financial ability to live a life of maintenance is complex, for most of us will have to work for a living. I would like to give you a list of what you must finance as a schizophrenic who is self-supporting:

- Doctor, medications, and medical insurance.
- The money to place a down payment on a house. This includes mortgage, household bills, taxes on property and house; and insurance for fire, flood, hurricane, or earthquake (this depends on the location of your home geographically).
- Car registration and car payments.

- Life insurance for your family.
- Food and heath products. Water bills and utilities.
- Yard maintenance and house maintenance.
- Disposal of trash.
- Savings and investments for emergency, this also includes retirement accounts because some day you may want to retire.
- If you have children there are even more expenses involved, your child's health and welfare. Also your child will need an education to have a chance to succeed and have a good life.

The list goes on. To break the stereotype of schizophrenia, it takes a great deal of effort and a plan.

I have an advantage, and I know this is my most important life decision: to finish college and try to complete a master's degree. I will receive money, but I must also continue to maintain a level of success with my grades to be accepted into a master's program. And to stay in the master's program also requires a minimum grade point average.

I hope that my list has not given you discouragement in your attempt to reach a self outside the expected stereotype the world has of schizophrenia. However, you can someday make all that it takes to fulfill life if you open the door of knowledge that is waiting for you at elementary, junior high, high school, and college. There are books in public and college libraries that give information on scholarships and grants. There is help almost for everyone.

I invite all schizophrenics today to accept the challenge to step into reality. There is an opportunity for every person who is schizophrenic to become a great success. The words of great men and women throughout the world are right before us; mentors to guide our lives. Never turn the opportunity for achievement down just because someone says you're a failure. I say proudly that you are gifted and amazing. Never let anyone lower your self-esteem by saying "you are schizophrenic." There is a world waiting for schizophrenics of all ages with intelligent brains that I believe some day the world will know.

Pass this valuable information on to all those that have schizophrenia. The time is now, and we must turn to success in this world by praise of ourselves to maintain self-esteem, and never doubt the most impossible task that others make you think in reality you can never achieve. Take the life of Helen Keller and share your triumph with Helen. Build your reliance on medication as a blessing, and focus on your ethical values to motivate you to fulfill your good desires.

Please understand what it is I am writing is in all sincerity, that I am not causing a new awakening for anyone, but truth based upon my own experience with patients, psychiatrists, psychologists, and mental health professionals who have shared with me the possibility to have a real plan for real success. Trust yourself, and take what words a friend and patient has written to motivate schizophrenics. I know it's hard now, but it only gets easier when you maintain on medication; God bless you all, my your payers be full of your desires of good to God.

So I give you words to carry you bravely on the path to success of life in this world: If we dwell over our mistakes, we have no courage and strength to face adversity. I lived with faith, and now have life to grow with God. I hope this thought will inspire your will to achieve all your desires that are good.

I have tried to relate in the past two paragraphs an example of how faith can motivate you and has the power to change your life. I am not writing that you must become clergy of a religion but rather the change comes when you reflect on God and then truth is thus established. You may wonder how to reflect on God.

I can tell you my method. I verbally praise and glorify God in the morning when I am out of bed. I explain to God that I am using the words "praise and glory" to worship him. I simply repeat the words vocally alone and then I tell Him he is the only "Holy God." Five times then I repeat these words, "praise and glory." Now if I pray that way, I know there are many of you in this world who can write a prayer in your own way to worship God. It changes your attitude for the whole day. For me, it reminds me to forgive myself and others, then I briefly confess my sins to God. I am no ordained theologian, but I find a way each day to confirm to God my truth to him. God listens and answers in many ways.

Sometimes when the sun is out but my room is shady, I ask Christ for truth and thank him and praise him, and sometimes the light becomes brighter in my room. This is the truth of my experience with Christ. What matters is you maintain a faith in life that is guided by a ethics based on good laws that give life rather than take it away. This faith is the structure of a healthy society. This faith also gives personal growth and development in establishing a plan in life.

This chapter reminds you that there is a definite stereotype for schizophrenics. There will be until the cause and the cure are discovered. Now that we have addressed some methods of changing thinking and symptoms of mental illness on the visual body, we build a new reality that keeps us aware of our self and keeps a routine check on our brain and body. There is nothing to fear in change if it can benefit you. I hope that more people will share with others the truth of their lives as schizophrenics. The more information we share, the more we open acceptance of what we cannot stop, which is the symptoms of schizophrenia. Each of us as schizophrenics must do our best to maintain medication and educate ourselves so that we may become self- supporting. We may be schizophrenics, but we can accomplish high levels of success in work, obtain an education in college, and regularly seek the wisdom and support from our psychiatrists and mental health professionals.

We must work to end the stereotype that has portrayed schizophrenics as dangerous. It is not true. Those who kill are criminals who have more complex disorders than the average schizophrenic. We must all help each other to become aware of how misunderstood is the diagnosis of the mental disorder of schizophrenia.

I would like to add that I encourage you to write some of your own experiences. As you have noticed, after each chapter I have included a page for your notes. I hope these pages will help you in recording your own experiences and information. I would also like to add that if you have the desire to write a book on schizophrenia, the information that you record may be used to brainstorm ideas that you can use to create a book as unique as your own experiences with schizophrenia. I believe you can write if you take the time and have the financial support to publish your book. It takes work, but when finished, you have something to gain and to give: sharing with others your own unique information. Your writing can greatly increase the world's understanding of schizophrenia. It's a great feeling when you have finally completed your book. I wish you the very best of success.

PART TWO

Work and Collect

Government programs offer assistance for schizophrenics: Social Security, disability benefits, Medicare, and others. Check with your government wherever you live. Did you know that you can work and pay taxes while continuing to collect Social Security? Working income is reported to Social Security, and there are restrictions on the amount of money you can earn; however, the income of work can help. If you receive benefits of $900 or more a month, you can earn at a job without penalty up to $800 a month gross. Be aware: the amount of eligible income may not be the net amount. The Social Security office that administers payments and maintains records of benefits may quote you a gross amount of earnings. The gross figure may be $800 a month in earnings, but it includes federal and state taxes, SSI, worker's comp, and possibly other expenses. So you would earn less actual take-home pay. Your gross may be $800 a month, but take-home in your pay check after deductions would be about $600. But this is only an estimate of possible earnings. The amount of income changes each year, so please check with your Social Security benefits case worker and ask the amount of money you may earn. You or your payee must report your earnings to Social Security if you have a change of income. They will also ask whether you are continually diagnosed with schizophrenia. Because there is no cure, you can have your physician or payee fill out the forms required by Social Security.

There are benefits to working, in addition to money. You can develop training experience while you are working. It's important to have good social skills. This is an opportunity to learn that you can do more for yourself than mope over the fact that you have a mental disorder. If you stay on your medication, there is no reason why you cannot work, unless your schizophrenia is severe. My advice to you is to do the tasks that your employer asks of you.

Never turn into the employee that people think is a problem; try to be the best employee you can be! How, you ask? By not getting into the gossip of work. Do your work with speed and accuracy. Do not complain. There are always some people who complain; don't be fooled that they are doing what is right. Your employer will appreciate your hard work and effort to get along with others.

When you get a job, it's best to keep silent about your mental illness. The reason is that there are going to be others who do not share the compassion that your psychiatrist and family or friends may have in your life. So trust me, keep the illness with your doctor and family. There are those who still fear mental illness.

Once you succeed at keeping a job, there is special housing for low income men and women who receive Social Security and work. The housing is at a discounted rate based on your income and expenses. If you are interested in learning more about independent living, I suggest that you call your local city housing authority. In incorporated cities in the United States, you can call your city hall and ask about independent living for low income men and women. Employees there can guide you into finding rentals in your area that are for low income. There may be a waiting list for available housing, so don't feel gloomy if you have to be placed on a waiting list. There will eventually be an opening for you, but don't be surprised if it may take up to two years in some major cities or small towns.

I have lived more than half of my life with schizophrenia. I am continually learning how to find my path in this world. I am, just like you, desiring a better life and money to help pay the bills. I have had many jobs and some I have chosen to leave. However, there has never been a word of resentment by me for the employers of the past.

If you are allowed to work, you may also be eligible for Medicare insurance. The system in different parts of the world is different. Check with your state and federal government to find out what social services your country has available. The above is in the United States and is only an estimate. There are some countries that offer reduced housing cost and coupons for receiving food assistance, and reduced or even free education based on income and grade point averages from high school. Many states in the US give grants to students who qualify by low income. I received a grant that paid for my classes at college based on my income. Check with the financial aid office of your local college.

I realize that physician visits and medication are extremely expensive. There are ways to receive free medication through drug companies by contacting the manufacturer of the medication you are taking. If you are taking medication and need a discount, go to your local pharmacy and talk with them and ask about assistance programs offered by drug companies based on income.

There is also the benefit of food stamps. These are available to anyone who is low income and receiving Social Security payments based on illness. Just call the local or state welfare office and tell them that you receive Social Security and your expenses of medication, which you will have to prove, make it unable for you to pay for food. They will base your benefit according to your Social Security benefit earnings sheet mailed to you or your payee. Please bring this document with you to the welfare office. They also may request that you show your last year's tax form, which shows your most current earnings. I highly recommend that you accept all the benefits you are entitled to receive as a man or woman with a permanent disability.

Also check assistance programs offered by local charities. Possibly your local, state, or federal government may not assist you with your permanent disability. If you cannot receive any benefits in your county, and there is a high prejudice against the mentally ill, you may want to contact a religious organization that can give you guidance to deal with your unique situation.

So let me review with you that you must find all the resources available to you for treatment of mental illness. I know there are some who will have severe schizophrenia and may require long-term mental health care at a hospital, but there are also some who will need only day treatment programs, and some in private care living without anyone knowing their diagnosis and are highly functional.

For now, in the U.S., there are many available sources of aid for schizophrenics. However I can say, depending on your national laws, you may live in a country that has advanced enough to recognize that there are many levels of severity of schizophrenia. Many can live a very functional life with schizophrenia.

I end by saying I know it may not seem fair that some people receive more than others, but find all ways that you can to better yourself in your own unique creative way.

Education

Although education may not be your choice in life, I encourage anyone who has the desire to learn and has the ability to be a student to earn a degree: a GED, or a junior college, college or university degree. If you have the ability to concentrate on listening to a teacher or professor for one or two hours, take notes, not disturb the class, and have a memory to recall information for exams, then you can succeed at a high school or college. You more than likely will always have homework and will be expected to write papers and participate in college exams. I know that high schools and colleges require that you maintain a minimal grade point average, or you will be terminated as a student. There is a lot of pressure to get reading assignments and papers or projects for your classes. Most students try hard to receive the highest GPA because transferring to a college in upper division is very competitive, and the students with the highest GPA are most likely to be accepted. But don't let all this hard work and effort keep you from attaining a college education. There is no better experience than receiving a degree.

When you apply for college admission, the college will require a high school transcript. You can call your high school and ask for your transcripts to be sent to the college of your choice. Some schools will ask you to pay a small fee. Then you fill out the application to the college. There are some colleges that require an essay with the application. There is also usually an application fee that covers the cost of admissions review. Most junior colleges are less expensive than four-year colleges and universities. More than likely you will need to apply for financial aid to cover the cost of your education. Help is available in scholarships, grants, and loans from the government and private lenders. It sounds like work; it is, but it is very rewarding. A great number of men and women who have had schizophrenia have earned university degrees. It's not uncommon to find schizophrenics earning post-graduate degrees.

Silence about your disease is also a good rule of choice in a college setting. I learned that when I kept quiet about schizophrenia, I did better than at previous colleges where I had shared my mental illness with a friend or a professor.

Once you get the routine down, there are plenty of social activities for the students at the school that you attend. This is also a great way to meet people in your new environment. There are many people who maintain these friendships after graduation. I say that this is the best way to find a career that you are interested in for your life.

Realize you are not a failure, however, if you choose not to receive an education. As I have mentioned before, you are unique and different than anyone else in the world, and that is a blessing enough in this life. I realize that as a schizophrenic, you may have a more difficult time than others because of the symptoms and the effects of medication, not to mention the personal problems that you have not yet resolved in your life. So whatever your decision is, know that you are going to achieve your very best. I would like to write that I know your best is unique and that you can feel calm and peace by knowing this.

As schizophrenics, we face a burden of our own. I would say that it's like carrying on bravely in the presence of adversity. But you don't need to be desperate. However difficult life is there are people who can assist you to help you cope with schizophrenia. I know that we're all unique, but staying on medication is the first priority to winning success with schizophrenia. This is the first step to becoming a self-maintaining man or woman. So remember, a good night's sleep can clear the brain. Begin each day as a new day in which you can change when you allow yourself to be fresh and new.

The Single Life

Single life with schizophrenia is common. But do not fear that you are alone with your mental illness. Life can be fulfilling as a single with schizophrenia. There are many activities that you can become involved with. For those who are able to live independently and maintain friendships, there are ways to grow and succeed in daily life.

One possibility might be getting into reading. There are books that can educate you, as well as books for only pleasure reading and entertainment. Reading a newspaper is common for most people, and it's good advice to read a newspaper to keep up your knowledge of what is going on in your area and the world. This practice will help keep your brain occupied, a good thing, even if you are like some readers who read the headlines and skim through the paper. There is a lot going on in this world, and being able to read is part of life, so if you find pleasure in reading, you just may learn something. Every type of book you can desire is available at different book stores. I have discovered that used book stores have a wide variety of inexpensive paperback and hard cover books available if you wish to own the book you are reading. Also, some of the major book chain stores have good sales on their merchandise throughout the year, and public libraries provide a wide assortment of books.

There are many beliefs in this world, but whatever your faith, I suggest that you develop it and find a place where men and woman believe like you. This is a good way of making friends and finding a place to share your faith. Whatever you choose to believe that is spiritual, you are entitled to have an opportunity to expand your spiritual belief.

If you cannot share it, then remember that you are not alone, and your belief is a freedom that no one can take that away. If you look in your local telephone book, most have listings of places to go to worship. I highly encourage you to attend the one of your choice. Being there gives you a form of community where you are protected with others of your same faith.

What about friendship? It's great to have the companionship of people who share your interests, people who are supportive and emotionally healthy. However, you don't need any "problem friends." Have you ever met someone who speaks only of problems? Can you imagine what is happening in this person's brain? This is not a healthy person, and the best way to keep yourself from developing a relationship as the ear that listens to all problems is to get away from the person. It's not you; it's the negative person who never changes, and believe me, twenty years down the road, the same personality will never change. What you must know is that it's a mental illness, so get out as quickly as possible. The fact that you are schizophrenic does not give any man or woman the right to load you down with dysfunction. Do yourself a favor and let that relationship end so you can turn your attention to happier pursuits. Do not be caught by a dysfunctional person who makes you appear to be the problem. That person is never going to change, and remember, you are not the one with a problem. You're the healthy one and receiving medication and therapy and psychiatric treatment. When you end that relationship, you have just one less problem, and who needs any more problems when you have schizophrenia?

It is important to realize that your associates and the friends you choose affect you in many ways. If you do not drink, smoke, or do drugs, would you surround yourself with people who do? If you want to think positively, surround yourself with people who solve their own problems. Find friends who treat you with the respect that you deserve. Life may offer you men and woman just like you who can help you by being examples and mentors.

I would like to now share some of my own life as a single, and what fulfillment I found when I had resolved all that I could not control. I could not make schizophrenia go away. I knew this was my cross. I am a Christian; this is the reason I know at forty-four how to live with this cross so that others will not have to have as difficult a time as I have dealing with schizophrenia. But I know, even though I have overcome some hard times mentally, I have been blessed. I have worked hard, and I am a man who has experienced low pay. But I managed to find a way to accept each job I held and make the best of it. When others would gossip, I would remain silent and not become part of the games played, those games that always fall on the honest one at work. My advice has come from years of experience. You can save yourself a lot of hardship by doing your work the best you can, and you will always feel the satisfaction that you did your best.

Living alone with the freedom to come and go as you like, to eat or sleep at odd hours, is a great feeling. As a bachelor, I can say it has been fun many times. Although I am still seeking that soul mate I would like to spend the rest of my life with in a marriage, I have not hidden myself away while I was waiting for her to show up. Dating as a single really is fun.

If you are good at choosing healthy men and women, then there is nothing to fear about having a steady relationship with someone. You do not have to commit to marriage, but can enjoy the path of dating and meeting new friends where you may find an exciting and fulfilling partnership. Choosing to be single is not being selfish. There is a big commitment in deciding to marry. But the wonderful part about single life is that you will have the opportunity to meet different types of men or woman. Bachelors or bachelorettes, you have the right to choose whom you like the most. When you find friends or a steady to be with, I encourage you to live with them to the fullest. There is nothing to fear about spending a little money on a relationship that is equal, where your friends or you take turns paying the bill.

As a single, you have a better chance of preserving your privacy by not mentioning your illness. Please understand there are many uneducated beliefs pertaining to schizophrenia. You are entitled to your privacy. Save your discussions for the men and women trained in mental illness. These men and woman will be more supportive with you about your mental illness.

Sports are also great fun for those who have the desire to maintain a healthy body. There are gyms or places such as parks to walk, jog, run, or bike. These activities are important for those of us who understand that food and exercise have proven to help us live longer and better.

Going to the gym three times a week and walking four times a week helps reduce cholesterol.

What do you eat? I know that many of you who will read this book may be going without a healthy diet based on many factors. Some of these factors may be money. There are, in many countries, food assistance programs that may help in providing you with supplies of food. Please find out where there is food for low-income disabled in your area. There is private and public funding available in many countries.

I would like to say that if you are single and desire to stay that way, there is nothing to be afraid of. Life can be full of happiness even if you are single. You are unique; so is your path of life.

Marriage

Marriage is a beautiful blessing in life. The vow to share life for better or worse, to commit for life a shared respect for one and another, to honor and protect each other through life with all its adversities. I believe that there is a natural drive for every man or woman to marry a companion some day.

There is nothing more glorious than the bonding that is in a marriage when two meet and begin sharing life as an equal opportunity to find the love deep within the soul. After all, this is what makes a marriage stay together: giving all, and when you cannot, your partner gives the love that is needed to maintain your vows.

It's work at times because we are human. We have emotions that, in our most vulnerable moments, fear a sharing of self. Yes, marriage is a risk, there is no doubting this. However, when you find your partner who shares many of the same beliefs and desires in life, then the true beauty of marriage becomes reality. One of the most wonderful blessings in a marriage is the bonding that comes within a marriage.

So, you're asking, what does this have to do with a schizophrenic? A lot of men and woman who are mentally ill have never experienced what a relationship is like. Until you finally find that soul mate, you may think it will never happen. Then it all comes to life, and a healthy pair meet! The road of marriage can also be for men and women who have schizophrenia; there is no law that says if you are schizophrenic that you cannot get married. Whether you find a man or woman who has a similar mental illness, or you meet someone who lovingly accepts your mental illness, life in a marriage takes giving your fullest to the one you have married. There is no easy method.

There is a great deal more to think about if you have made the decision to begin those exciting wedding plans to legalize your happiness, joy, and love for each other! But never forget that as a schizophrenic, you must be completely truthful with your future spouse. There are going to be times when you may wish time alone after a day of work, and you must plan for all the different types of behavior you may have on the days that you hear voices.

Now remember, being aware of yourself will hide what is going on inside your brain. So be the best actor you can be in life! Nonetheless, even while you are living an abundant and beautiful life, there are going to be times when the effects of your medication become of great concern. So please consult your psychiatrist and your physical doctor to discuss what you as a schizophrenic can plan for as a family.

Whatever decision you make, know that any medication being taken by a man or woman can cause fetal deformity. When I was studying to be a pharmaceutical technician, I studied medications—and whatever anyone tells you, I know that there is a high risk of deformity with over the counter and prescription medications. Check with your doctor, and have some medical tests on the effects of medications that could affect you. As always, none is best. But if you are schizophrenic, you will probably want to increase your number of sessions with your psychiatrist to maintain normality.

Your doctors may advise you that you cannot have children or that you should not risk having children, either because of your medication or because of a genetic component in your mental illness. You should discuss with your beloved how you feel about an alternative approach. You might consider adoption or foster care.

I hope that my chapter on self-awareness has helped you to know what your smile looks like, or an angry face that I encourage you to never show, but when you are sad or depressed, try to imagine what you look like when you do not take your medication! There are going to be times to observe how you stand, what else are you doing standing? Do you look masculine or feminine when you stand? How about when you speak; do you move your hands in making visual cues, or do you leave your arms to your side, or put them in your pocket? All of what I have explained is to assist you in becoming aware of what you do when you have symptoms of schizophrenia and you are in a relationship where you will be observed every day by your wife or husband.

If you are not prepared with knowledge on the inside that affects gestures on the outside, do you understand how that would be something to work on to control your visual presence? If you do not know when a symptom is coming on, you will need to practice to keep your appearance in compliance with the expectations of an average man or woman. You want to work on being as unnoticeable as possible. It is hard work, but it makes you appear more normal than schizophrenics that do not use this technique. When you are in public, observe a visual gesture that you see someone make, or pay attention to their look in clothes. These exercises may help you to fit into the normal look of men and woman.

I would like to add that when you are married, you will probably continue working, and the main reason is that the money can be one of the biggest problems in marriages, sometimes even causing them to fail. It's tough to have a marriage and have no money to support yourselves in a financially-based system. So really sit together and make a list of each of your individual income needs and then write your marriage expenses. At least one of you must make a very good income from a job to pay the expenses to support a family.

With all my heart I hope that if marriage is your dream, then may it be blessed with ways to earn and maintain together, and never have the desire to separate. It is important to be truthful and have faith in God, and when you take that vow believe it to be a promise to God. You can accomplish this if you give yourself a financially accurate plan to work between the two of you in your relationship.

You really believe and think, *Do I love this man or woman enough to overcome this disorder?* whether it is one or both who suffer from schizophrenia. A major part of this commitment is based on the social skills needed and the amount of trust to not feel isolated because there are good days and bad days, and you cannot skip work just because you feel bad or are suffering. You have to overcome the hard days, and that requires that you remember you have jointly agreed to give all when your partner needs you. There are going to be difficult days and nights ahead of you due to your schizophrenia. But it is possible to be married, to live a successful marriage, and to show the world that you beat the odds. God bless you both.

I would like to share with you that (as I have written previously) medication for a schizophrenic is expensive, and you need to commit to it all your life. This is the main and only successful way to have a chance of ever being married. Do your best, and when you get an education or trade, continue the job until you have enough money saved to retire in a good way. Think about health care and Social Security. The amount of money you will need is measured by the dream of how well off you want to be. Would you like to spend money traveling around the world, or golfing on the course near your house, or maybe vacationing at a house at the beach? This is all going to cost money and you will still need money beyond this amount to give to your family when you pass over to heaven.

If you are thinking about getting married, you should consider counseling with a psychiatrist and a marriage and family counselor. This way the two of you will have a chance to learn how to react to the partner who has schizophrenia and what to expect, and the joint cooperation that you both will need because the only treatment is medication. There are many psychiatrists and psychologists who approve of the marriage between a schizophrenic and a partner who is not schizophrenic. You just need the right amount of time and may consider bi-yearly counseling to help with your marriage. With medication all will be well. If you have found someone to love, there is a good chance all will go well.

There is no other relationship like marriage. It's more than living with someone. It's deciding that for the rest of your life you will commit your life to the betterment of another. It's the most intimate relationship you will ever have. I realize that there are a great number of divorces, but you can make your marriage work if it is healthy, both mentally and physically. I believe that the reason marriages fail is that people forget their vows. Also there may not be enough maturity in both partners to keep going through the difficult times. Think to yourself, *Is this man or woman that I am going to marry mentally healthy?* Then ask yourself, *Am I healthy enough to marry someone and maintain through the difficult times that I have no control over?* Marriage, yes, is good for the soul and body. But do not believe you are ready for marriage if you have to lie to yourself about personality traits that a future partner may have; they will drive you crazy all of your marriage.

There are also people who just cannot live without being married. This is not a healthy mind. It's compromise every day of your life. When two such partners join to live their lives together, and I know from many men and women who have been this way, they eventually throw in the towel, and set off to find someone else. But there are further complications, such as they never really take time to evaluate their lives to learn the warning signs of the past so that there is no repeat. Why do they not consider counseling before the attempt to continue in another relationship? The truth is they may not believe they contributed to any of the problems in their marriage. They are still blaming the other partner for the past failed marriage. The truth is that the next relationship carries this unhealthy anger from the past marriage. Who wants to hear how bad your last relationship was? I am sure if you have resolved the conflict and are healthy, the marriage excludes past failed marriages.

Because men and women have different chemistry in their bodies, know that sometimes we just do not feel and think the same. This is going to lead to conflict unless you know that sometimes we do not agree but say to yourselves, "Let's work this out in a healthy way, no argument, just both of us can compromise." This is good and healthy. I see in many relationships how anger is used in communication and I find this to be very disturbing. One is being a giver, and the angry partner is a taker; take time to evaluate this type of situation because if there is anger, then there is a need for therapy to find out why you are living a life in turmoil. More than likely people say to themselves, "Oh, my partner is just like that," or "We are having a bad day." The truth is there is something that needs change, and an angry partner more than likely needs years of therapy before there will be change. So get out of an abuser-of-marriage relationship. It's a marriage that is doomed for failure.

There are marriages that are healthy. But before you tie the knot, ask yourself, *Do I have any problems that need resolving before I make the decision to marry?* The way to success is being free of problems before you marry, not after. Do not fool yourself into thinking that marriage is going to solve your problems. There is enough compromise involved within marriage that you need all the good you can obtain in marriage.

Now that I have briefly mentioned marriage in its success and potential failures, I still believe that you must start out right—no secrets, lies, or past problems—before you become married. If both partners can do this then the best relationship you have ever dreamed is about to become reality. If you have a plan that you both agree upon before you get married, and you can trust each other to live by this and your original vows, I believe you are beginning the path to a healthy marriage.

In Closing

In closing this book, I would like to say if you're a patient, parent, sibling, or other relation, maybe a friend, doctor, or mental health professional, I want to say thank you for reading and sharing my book. I truly believe that anyone with schizophrenia deserves my heart of compassion. I find that there is a great deal of information available about schizophrenia, some professional and some written by patients. I hope to help other patients have a connection with a writer; you can relate to as a patient with schizophrenia. I hope that you have gained some knowledge from my experiences. I hope you find joy in finding that there is finally someone to relate to who is just an average man who has written a book to help others. If anything, you may have found insight to overcome the desire to stop medication.

This book has come from my brain and my own experience, along with the guidance of my own psychiatrist, Dr. Lisa Schmid, M.D. I switched doctors often during the course of my illness and struggling with control issues, until I finally found a doctor who understands my ambition to succeed. Her pride in my accomplishments gives me confidence to work.

For those of you who normally do not read, I hope you have a feeling of accomplishment by finishing reading this book.

I now can take a moment to recap some of the key topics I have discussed in the first part this book. First, take your medication whether you think it is working or not. The facts are, the longer you stay on medication, the stronger chances you have to relieve yourself of abnormalities associated with schizophrenia. So please stay on your medication and take it as directed by your psychiatrist. This is the number one thing you as a patient can do to improve your quality of your life.

Second, depression is a serious mental illness. It can leave you with horrible a down feeling. However, there is hope. The medications are advancing, and the treatment is improving. Get the help you need with a psychiatrist, mental health counseling, or a licensed mental health professional to overcome your depression.

The next chapter that I would like to highlight is on voices. I have revealed that voices are not really someone else speaking to you. Schizophrenics all have this delusion. The sooner you believe that they are not anyone else, the sooner you will place yourself into reality. Voices are something we as schizophrenics must live with, remembering that they are really not a friend or enemy. There is no ESP from someone else to you as a schizophrenic.

Hallucinations are next. I have discussed that many times in a schizophrenic's life there is a chance that you will hallucinate, and the truth is it's just like everything else. It's a false reality, and there is no truth to hallucinations. For the most part, going off medication can cause you to hallucinate and believe its reality. There is a possibility that even if you are on medication you may hallucinate, but the truth is that you have a better chance of believing that they are not reality on medication. So whatever you see and hear, the best method of treatment is to continue taking your medication. If it persists, please consult your psychiatrist and mental health professional to establish the reality that this is a symptom of schizophrenia.

In the next chapter, I gave you fictitious situations about paranoia. Although they may be imaginary, there is something to learn from these situations. Most paranoid schizophrenics are not taking their medication. This is one sure way to end up in a mental hospital. If you stop taking your medication, you run the risk of becoming paranoid.

Dealing intelligently and responsibly with these symptoms will allow you to overcome the stereotypes of schizophrenia and to become a successful and self-reliant individual.

There is nothing that is going to keep you from God, and life holds some difficulty for everyone. You just were born with schizophrenia. Think in your brain for a moment how easy life can really be when we make an attempt to realize that we have a mental illness, but we also have highly trained professionals in the mental health field to assist us in dealing with it. The benefit is that we have it pretty easy, and we didn't have to become psychiatrists to deal with our own mental illness. Mental health treatment has been around a lot longer than your life, and it's only going to improve over time.